Pathway to Purely His

"5 Steps to Go ALL IN & Get UNSTUCK"

By Michelle E. Caswell

aBM

Published by:

A Book's Mind

PO Box 272847

Fort Collins, CO 80527

www.abooksmind.com

Copyright © 2016

ISBN: 978-1-944255-20-6

Printed in the United States of America

A Letter from the Author

I am so excited about the journey you're about to embark on! I just know that the Lord has amazing plans for your life and He is going to use this group as a launching pad for your future. Thank you for taking the leap of faith and committing five months of your life to being a part of this Purely His group.

Please keep in mind that everything I will be sharing throughout this workbook are all things that come from my own personal story. Please know that I have traveled the same journey that you are about to embark on and I would never ask you to do something that I wasn't willing to do myself. Just remember, it is not going to be easy, but it will be worth it!

The goal of a Purely His group is for you to 'go all in with Jesus and get unstuck from anything in the way of that' by using these five steps to get there. The five steps are as follows:

#1 Your Story, #2 His Story, #3 Get Unstuck, #4 Walk it Out, #5 Take Someone with You

Your group time will produce results, because you will do more than just sit around and talk about issues: you will confront them, work through them and heal from them. This will result in being able to move on to becoming all that the Lord has uniquely called you to be.

I want you to be aware that you will face spiritual opposition from the enemy as you begin pursuing the Lord with everything you have! Do not be surprised by it when it happens. Just know that it's coming and resist him by not giving up or giving in. *"Submit yourselves, then, to God. Resist the devil, and he will flee from you."* James 4:7

I know that you are going through this process for yourself, but God doesn't want you to keep it to yourself. He eventually wants you to give it away. He wants you to help others. We all have our own circle of influence, specific people that you can reach and specific people that I can reach. However, if we all work together, think how quickly we can turn our families, communities and the world upside down! So won't you join me in this discipleship movement that God has called us to?

It's no accident or coincidence that you are here. God chose you. Thank you for taking the risk to join this group. I encourage you to keep taking risks, because your life is about to completely change.

I sure hope to meet you someday if I haven't already,

Michelle E. Caswell

Founder of Purely His, Inc.

Testimonials of PH Group Members

"When I came into Purely His I didn't have high expectations that it would do anything for me, but it turned out to be very powerful in turning my life around and also my walk with God."–Steve

"I stepped into Purely His a total skeptic, and stepped out a totally different person. It really works!" Karen

"Purely His has been a Godsend for me. Matt and Michelle truly have the heart of the Father in caring for the Body of Christ. Being in a group and then leading my own, the Lord has both dealt with deep things in me and also drawn me closer to Him in ways I never expected." -Josh

"Purely His is a community of sisters who help you to drop your mask, become real, and get free from your wounds of the past. It is only then that we can "walk the walk" with Jesus." Christa

"Purely His is all about being set free and staying free...being ALL in with Jesus." –Bob

"During those times of walking through my deepest pain, I find my first reaction is to run right out the door. Being vulnerable is not my thing BUT I encourage you to push through it! Peace, hope, and JOY are all waiting there to envelop you! The healing is so worth it." Charmaine

"I believed wearing a mask was the only way to be accepted until Purely His. Jesus came to set us free from the guilt and shame of our pasts and now I know what freedom feels like." Cynthia

"Trust the process. Consistency is so important. Show up every week, rain or shine. Be brave and honest and vulnerable and do the work. The change is worth it." Jenna

"Life changing. Made true friends that will last a lifetime. Got to be real and felt safe doing it. Loved, accepted, treasured, and took risks to grow. Dumped old baggage, learned to walk in forgiveness. Learned how to trust again. No longer walking in fear!!!" Kimberly

Table of Contents

Group Contact List

Name   Phone   Email

_____

_____

_____

_____

_____

_____

_____

_____

_____

_____

_____

_____

_____

_____

_____

Week 1-Meet & Greet

The leaders just shared...they went first, dropped their masks and kept it real.

1. Are you surprised by their stories?

_____

_____

_____

_____

_____

_____

2. Could you relate to them personally?

_____

_____

_____

_____

_____

_____

3. What are some of your fears and hopes for the next 5 months?

_____

_____

_____

_____

_____

_____

My Pledge to Our Group

___**I will drop my mask and keep it real.** This is a place where I will be honest and authentic; I will not pretend to be who I think I should be or who others think I should be.

___**Your secrets are safe with me.** What happens in the group, stays in the group. The ONLY exception to breaking confidentiality is if someone is in danger of harming themselves or another person. In that case, I will inform the leader of my group so they can handle the situation accordingly. Many of us will be coming into the group with trust issues. It is a risk that we are all going to have to take in order to experience the freedom and healing that we are striving towards. *Gossiping to anyone* (including spouses) *cannot and will not be tolerated.*

___ **I will not judge you.** Although we are coming from different backgrounds, we are headed in the same direction. I will hear confessions or discussions that may shock/offend me and possibly make me uncomfortable, but I will do my best to respond gently. I will be aware of my body language and facial expressions as they can unintentionally communicate judgment. I want to love people out of their sin, not condemn them in it.

___ **I am willing to deal with the root cause.** The purpose of this group is to help you go all in with Jesus and to help you get unstuck from anything that may stand in the way of that. I am willing to look at the root cause(s) of my current struggles, and/or my lack of passion for the Lord.

___**We will mentor each other.** This is a group effort so I will participate and get involved. Contributing to this group experience will give me the tools and skills to mentor one on one, or to facilitate a group of my own.

___ **I will not give up and I will respect your time.** I understand how busy life can be, but I commit to being on time and ready to dive in each week. The five steps build on each other, so it really is important to attend every class. We only have 5 months together - *time will go very fast!*

___ **I will give others a chance to speak.** Some of us will be more reserved and quiet, and will have to challenge ourselves to step out of our comfort zone and speak up! There are also those of us that like to talk, and, well, you may need to stick a cork in it!

Date: _____You have my word, _____

MICHELLE E. CASWELL   PURELY HIS, INC.

Week 2-Step 1 Your Story

*"I praise you because I am fearfully and wonderfully made; Your works
are wonderful, I know that full well."*

Psalm 139:14

<u>Step 1: Your Story</u> (Refer to pages 48-58 in Calling All Workers)

Have you ever questioned who you truly are, and what your purpose on this earth actually is? There are those that have made finding the answers to those questions the greatest quest of their life. Fortunately for you, the journey you are about to begin is one of self-discovery and understanding. Soon you will find the answers by discovering who you actually are, who you are in Christ, and the truth about who He made you to be.

To begin this process, focus your mind and think back to when you were a little kid. Think about how you acted, how you dressed, what you dreamed of being, how you liked to play, and the feelings you felt *before* tragedy or hard times hit your life. Remember back, before the abuse, divorce, let downs, and abandonment. Why is this important?

Because that is the real you...your real identity...the one God made.

Regrettably, the world around us makes us into something we're really not. When I am working with someone or self-reflecting, I try to envision who they were as a little child prior to all the stuff happening. I try to see the real person underneath all the junk that got piled on top. They are still in there. You are still in there. As you progress through the steps of Purely His, we are going to help you get free from the lies, labels, and addictions that are covering up the real you. Once that is done, you will be able to see who God made you to be and will rediscover the real you. This step is so important, so take your time and go deep.

We start with who you are right now, then we talk about who you used to be, and who you dream of being in the future. Because somewhere mixed in with your past, present and future is the real you. Try not to be scared! Just be as real and honest as you possibly can, and let us help you discover YOU again.

When I came out of a six year abusive relationship, someone asked me, *"Michelle, who are you?"* and I answered, *"If you want me to be honest, I don't know. I feel like I am upside down and inside out. I have no idea who I am or what I like anymore"*. And maybe that's your story at this point. But *that is not my story any longer*, and soon it won't be yours either!

You did not go through everything for nothing. There is a reason you survived all the tragedies. God is going to heal you and He is going to use you, <u>if you let Him</u>. Everything you have gone through will not go to waste. In fact **Your Story** will be your authority; it will be your platform. It may be hard to believe, but the things you are most ashamed of right now will most likely be the things that God uses to set a lot of people free. So be courageous, do your best to drop your mask, keep it real, and allow the others in your group to speak into your life, the truths they see about you.

Building Real Relationships

"And let us consider how we may spur one another on toward love and good deeds, not giving up meeting together, as some are in the habit of doing, but encouraging one another—and all the more as you see the Day approaching."

Hebrews 10:24-25 (NIV)

Look around at those in this group, you may be strangers now, but that's all about to change. It's hard, if not impossible, to connect on a deep level when conversations are superficial-but this group will be anything but that.

Getting to know each other at a deep level like this will help everyone grow rapidly, especially if you will commit to holding each other accountable inside and outside of group time. To get healthy and stay healthy, you need to have people up in your business that know your struggles and are bold enough to call you out when they see you going in the wrong direction. Accountability is also really good for encouragement. When people really know what you want in life, they can encourage you towards your heart's desire. I'm sure you all have an area in your life that you want to get free from, so let others help you with that-together we can do this.

There's no sense in wasting time, let's jump right into it by 'dropping our masks and keeping it real.' Keep in mind that we're not here to compete with each other or act like we're in a better place than where we really are. We want to cultivate an environment where you can truly be yourself. Let's take a few minutes to start getting to know each other. Do your best to actively listen while others share, instead of thinking about what you are going to say next.

A struggle is a symptom of a deeper issue-THE issue

Let's Talk About It

1. Describe yourself...who are you? Tell us something about yourself that others wouldn't normally guess.

_____

_____

_____

_____

_____

2. What struggle are you hoping to get free from over the next several months?

_____

_____

_____

_____

_____

3. What is your motivation in being a part of this group? Example: *"I want to get married someday and not carry all this baggage into that relationship."* Or *"I want to work in ministry someday and be emotionally healthy so I can succeed at it."* Or *"I just want to feel better"*

_____

_____

_____

_____

_____

Let's Take Action

Homework

- Take a look at the list of scriptures below. Circle the ones you **don't** believe or are failing to walk out in your life currently. Look up the scriptures in your Bible and mark them. Take a few minutes to read the scriptures in your Bible that you do not currently believe and ask the Lord to help you with your unbelief.
- Contact one person in your group by text, email or a phone call.

Your Story

I am righteous and holy. (Ephesians 4:24)

I am saved by grace not by my performance. (Ephesians 2:8)

I have been made new in Him. (2 Corinthians 5:17)

I am full of light. (Matthew 5:14)

I am royalty. (1 Peter 2:9)

God has a good plan for me. (Ephesians 2:10)

I have great worth. (1 Corinthians 6:20)

I am right with God. (Hebrews 9:14)

My sins do not define me. (Matthew 26:28)

I am blameless. (Hebrews 10:17)

Nothing can separate me from His love. (Romans 8:35)

I am righteous. (Romans 5:17)

I have heavenly power. (Ephesians 2:6)

I can overcome anything. (Romans 8:37)

I am accepted. (Romans 15:7)

MICHELLE E. CASWELL   PURELY HIS, INC.

Let's Reflect

What are you feeling after realizing these things or talking about them?
What is the Lord showing you about your story?

_____

_____

_____

_____

_____

_____

_____

_____

_____

_____

_____

_____

_____

_____

_____

_____

_____

_____

_____

Week 3- The Real You

"Rather let it be the <u>hidden</u> person of the heart, with the <u>incorruptible</u> beauty of a gentle and quiet spirit, which is very precious in the sight of God." 1 Peter 3:4 (NKJV)

Let's look at last week's homework. Which verses did you circle and what happened in your past to make you not believe those scriptures?

There are reasons why you don't believe what the Bible says is true about who you are. Your reasons usually stem from past experiences. Get into the habit of asking yourself *"Why don't I believe this and what happened to make me not believe it?"* Your answer will usually point you to the place where you are stuck.

Most of us have not liked our self at one time or another and some of us have good reason for even despising who we have become, but here's what I want you to know. The way that God originally created you was perfect, in fact in Psalm 139 it says, *"I am <u>fearfully</u> and <u>wonderfully</u> made."* Wouldn't it be amazing to actually believe that about yourself?

You see, the real you, the <u>hidden person</u> of your heart, is covered up by layers of junk that consist of wounds, labels, lies and unresolved issues. In order to get unstuck, you need to get rid of those layers so that you can be the REAL you again-the one God perfectly created.

Just remember that everyone comes in this group with baggage that needs to be unpacked. Your group time is a safe place to unpack it and leave it. We are here to carry each other's burdens, but the key is; to carry them to the cross, not home with us. We all have enough problems of our own, so let's not take anyone else's problems home with us, instead let's pray and hand them over to the Lord, so He can take care of them. His shoulders are plenty big enough for ALL of our problems.

**We are here to carry each other's burdens, but the key is;
to carry them to the cross, not home with us.**

Let's Talk About It

1. What was your relationship like with your parents as you were growing up? How did they interact with you?

_____

_____

_____

_____

_____

2. Who were you as a little kid? What did you like to wear, play and dream of being when you grew up?

_____

_____

_____

_____

_____

3. If you could do ANYTHING now and get paid for it, what would you do? (If money, education and location were not a hindrance.)

_____

_____

_____

_____

_____

MICHELLE E. CASWELL   PURELY HIS, INC.

Let's Take Action

Homework

- Make a list of who you are deep down inside. Hint: who were you as a child prior to the trauma you experienced? Then make another list of who you pretend to be or who you have become to protect yourself. **Example: I was a happy-go-lucky, optimistic kid who was trusting of people, but as an adult I was suspicious, cunning, and acted tougher than I really was.**

- Contact one person in this group by text, email or phone call and share something that you realized about yourself.

Real Life Example of someone I mentored. The real her was not nurtured, but rejected, abandoned and abused, so she decided that she needed to change herself to be accepted and to survive through life.

After I had her write this list I asked her to look at the real side and make the choice to accept herself just the way God made her. She discovered that she really liked the real her and has decided to 'drop the mask' and start walking out her real identity-the REAL her.

Here is an example of her list:

Real Me	Masked Me
Approachable	Intimidating
Empathetic	Apathetic
Peacemaker	Quick to Anger
Sees the best in people	Sees the flaws in people
Non-judgmental	Judgmental
Real Talk	Small Talk
Patient	Impatient
Perceptive to others needs	Self-seeking
Thoughtful in making decisions	Impulsive

Notice how they are complete opposites.

Now write your list.

Real You

Masked You

Let's Reflect

What are you feeling or experiencing after sharing these things? What is the Lord showing you about you and your story?

_____

_____

_____

_____

_____

_____

_____

_____

_____

_____

_____

_____

_____

_____

_____

_____

_____

_____

MICHELLE E. CASWELL   PURELY HIS, INC.

Week 4-Drop the Mask

"If God is for us, who can be against us?" Romans 8:31

Let's open up to our homework from last week. What did you notice about the Real You and the Masked You?

Learning to be a person of integrity, where your inside matches your outside, takes trust in God and acceptance of how He has uniquely made you. Many of us desperately seek others' approval and as long as they approve of us, we feel valued. If this approval is removed, our value diminishes.

It's time to start being okay with who you REALLY are and begin the journey of believing that the Lord already approves of you and unconditionally loves you. When you believe that kind of truth about yourself then there will be NO reason to wear a mask because you will know that you are good enough for the Creator of the World!

Getting your group to go deeper and connect in a real way takes effort from every participant. This journey really begins when you start 'dropping your mask and keeping it real'. Take the risk of being vulnerable by allowing others to see the junk you have been hiding behind your mask and the dreams tucked deep in your heart.

What you are going to find out is that you are a pretty awesome person and you're probably really going to like yourself, believe it or not. Get free by being the real you. It's so much easier to live life that way anyways, but you have to take the first step. You will have many opportunities in this group to practice in a safe environment and before you know it, 'keeping it real' will be a lifestyle for you.

It's important that you are able to see the mask you are wearing so you can drop it. A mask is where your outside appears different than what is really going on inside of you. (A mask is who you pretend to be, it's fake or a cover up.)

Types of Masks:
- Tough Girl
- Tough Guy
- Perfect
- Nothing special
- I'm OK
- Innocent

Let's Talk About It

1. What mask are you hiding behind?

_____

_____

_____

_____

_____

2. Why do you have a mask? What are you afraid of?

_____

_____

_____

_____

_____

3. What do you need to change in order to accept yourself more?

_____

_____

_____

_____

_____

MICHELLE E. CASWELL   PURELY HIS, INC.

Let's Take Action

Homework

- Focus this week on dropping your mask (wall of protection) and be vulnerable for as long as you can, as often as you can. Challenge yourself to be vulnerable longer each time. Being vulnerable doesn't always mean to cry or share your hurts, it can also mean to share your dreams for the future or how you really feel about something.

- Contact one person and share what your mask has been.

Who did you contact and what did you share?

_____

_____

_____

_____

_____

_____

Let's Reflect

What are you feeling or experiencing after sharing these things? What is the Lord showing you about you and your story?

_____

_____

_____

_____

_____

_____

_____

_____

_____

_____

_____

_____

_____

_____

_____

_____

MICHELLE E. CASWELL   PURELY HIS, INC.

Week 5-Step 2 His Story

"But who do you say that I am?"

"You are the Christ, the Son of the living God."

Matthew 16:15-16

Step 2: His Story (Refer to Page 58-66 in Calling All Workers)

Over the next several weeks you will be discovering His Story and how it has intertwined with Your Story. This step is all about meeting you right where you're at in your relationship with God. We don't want to assume that you are in a better place than where you really are, nor do we want to assume that you have a real relationship with God. We want you to be real about what your relationship with Him looks like, what it used to look like, and what you want it to look like. This step is similar to step 1, only this time it's in relation to God.

This process takes being real with your perceptions of Him. You might be surprised to find that other people in your group feel the same way you do. In Purely His, it's OK to be mad at God. It's OK to feel disappointed by Him. It's OK to not believe in Him. This is going to be a safe place for everyone to talk about those things.

We do hope that at some point, you make the decision to go 'all in' with Jesus; making Him your #1, your first love, and deciding to have an awesome, dynamic relationship with Him. That is our greatest hope for you-but we understand that you might not be at that place yet and that is totally fine.

I think it's really important for you to know what your story has been with Him: When did you first hear about Him, what changed your perspective, and what do you really want your relationship to look like with Him? These are things that are really important for you to know. The Bible says that we should *"be quick to give an answer for the hope that you have in Jesus Christ."* 1 Peter 3:15

We want that for you-to have that hope. Again, we understand you might not be there at this time, but we're going to get there together. It doesn't matter what background you come from or what your faith journey has been so far. What matters, is how you finish and we want you to finish strong.

Let's look at who God really is and how He really sees you. Try to have an open mind and heart while you're looking into these things about God.

Who is God to you?

"The Lord is compassionate and gracious, slow to anger, abounding in love." Psalm 103:8

How was it last week, with trying to drop your mask and keep it real? Who were you able to try out being vulnerable with? How did it go?

The Lord describes Himself in a way that most of us would not. However, God is not a liar, so is it possible that our perception is inaccurate? How we perceive God dictates our walk with Him. If we think of Him as angry, we will fear Him. If we see Him as distant, we will feel abandoned by Him. If we see Him as loving, then we will stop searching for love in all the wrong places.

Sometimes we put the image of a flawed human onto the face of God. Does God's personality remind you of anyone in your life? Your father, mother, spouse, grandmother? If you discover that you have been confusing a human with God's personality, consider starting over with God and getting to know the real Him.

The other circumstance that can warp our view of God can be when bad things happen to those we love, to ourselves or when we make bad choices. However, the truth is that He never changes, only our perception changes. Hebrews 13:8 *"Jesus Christ is the same yesterday and today and forever."*

Today we're going to get real about who God is to us. For those that were raised in a Christian home this may be more difficult for you because you know the right answers. However, do you walk out what you know? Knowing the right answers and living out those answers are two very different things.

Don't assume that someone is saved, just because they are in a Christian group, own a Bible, run a ministry or grew up in a Christian home. Being saved is about having a personal relationship with Jesus, not a religion.

MICHELLE E. CASWELL   PURELY HIS, INC.

Let's Talk About It

1. What is your faith?

_____

_____

_____

_____

2. What does God think of you and what do you think of Him?

_____

_____

_____

_____

3. When you picture God, what does His facial expression look like when He looks at you?

_____

_____

_____

_____

4. Name one good and bad experience you've had with God.

_____

_____

_____

_____

Let's Take Action

Homework

- Look at the "His Story" scripture list below and circle the ones that you don't believe or that you don't walk out in your life.
- Look up the scriptures that you circled in your Bible and mark them.
- Contact one person from the group and tell them one scripture you circled and what happened to make you not believe that particular scripture.

His Story

He is my defender. (Psalm 68:5)

He never gets tired of us. (Isaiah 40:28)

He is my provider. (Philippians 4:19)

He understands everything. (Isaiah 40:28)

He is perfect in every way. (Matthew 5:48)

He is compassionate. (Exodus 34:6)

He doesn't abandon us. (Deuteronomy 31:6)

He is not easily angered. (Exodus 34:6)

He never changes. (Hebrews 13:8)

He is faithful. (Exodus 34:6)

He is perfect love. (1 John 4:8)

He turns bad things into good. (Romans 8:28)

He wants to help us. (Isaiah 41:10)

He is patient. (Psalm 86:15)

He died for me personally. (Romans 5:8)

He is a good Father to everyone. (Ephesians 4:6)

MICHELLE E. CASWELL   PURELY HIS, INC.

Let's Reflect

What are you feeling or experiencing after talking about these things? What is the Lord showing you about you and your story with God?

_____

_____

_____

_____

_____

_____

_____

_____

_____

_____

_____

_____

_____

_____

_____

_____

_____

_____

MICHELLE E. CASWELL   PURELY HIS, INC.

Week 6-Your Unique Calling

"Your gifts and calling are irrevocable" Romans 11:29

Last week's homework was to circle the scriptures about God that you do not believe or walk out in your life. Which ones did you circle and why?

We want you to be living your life with purpose, so let us help you discover what your unique mission is. God has given us all a special heart for specific people groups like: children, single moms, homeless, elderly, etc. The reason is because God has a desire to save the whole world, so He gave us all a different heart for different people groups so that we could reach the world with Him in our own circle of influence.

You haven't missed your calling or opportunity to be used by Him. He has gifted you and has a special plan for your life. He is actually equipping you right now to go out and do just that. Your story is going to be your authority, your platform to be able to minister to others like only a person who "gets it" can. The best way to reach a drug addict is through an ex addict. The best person to help the homeless is someone who has been there-done that.

However, sometimes God calls His people to minister to those whose circumstances they can't relate to. But His spirit enables them to be effective anyways, so don't discount yourself just because your story is not the same as those you have a heart for.

It's so important that we get healthy, so we can go out and reach the world in our circle of influence for His honor and glory. It's pretty hard to focus on others when we are buried in our own junk.

You may be surprised to know that many of your strengths are actually spiritual gifts that the Lord has given you to do His work in this world. *"For we are God's handiwork, created in Christ Jesus to do good works, which God prepared in advance for us to do"* (Ephesians 2:10). Every gift is important, no gift is better than another and they are all needed and useful. Some people get envious of others' gifts, but steer away from that because nothing good can come out of that. Be thankful for the gift that God has blessed you with and be confident in knowing it was divinely chosen just for you!

Everyone has a dream in their heart that God placed there; it may be pushed down, forgotten or not realized, but it's there.

Let's Talk About It

1. If you could help any type of person anywhere in the world, who would it be?

_____

_____

_____

_____

2. What are your strengths and weaknesses?

_____

_____

_____

_____

3. What have you overcome in your life that could help someone else?

_____

_____

_____

_____

Let's take a spiritual gift test and discover how God uniquely made you.

MICHELLE E. CASWELL   PURELY HIS, INC.

Let's Take Action

Homework

- Give yourself permission to start dreaming and praying about His plan for you. Then journal what comes to your mind and heart. This is where child-like faith comes in. Just dream, don't interrupt the process by saying, "Oh, it's too late." or "How could I ever do that?"

- Contact one person and share your dream or share that you don't have one yet.

Let's Reflect

What are you feeling after sharing these things? What is the Lord showing you about your calling or dream for your life?

_____

_____

_____

_____

_____

_____

_____

_____

_____

_____

_____

_____

_____

_____

_____

_____

_____

_____

Week 7- The Blame Game

"Be alert and of sober mind. Your enemy, the devil prowls around like a roaring lion looking for someone to devour." 1 Peter 5:8

The main goal of Purely His is to help you 'go ALL IN with Jesus,' but that will be difficult if not impossible, IF you are holding a grudge against Him. I find it interesting that most people (including myself) immediately blame God for the BIG disappointments and hurts in our lives, but we don't blame the Enemy. Why is that?

Have you ever considered that the things you're holding against God are actually things that should be blamed on the Devil? There is a real enemy of our souls and we need to recognize that he is to blame for the evil in this world. Of course there is also man's free will and people are responsible for their own choices, however, I've noticed that people are being used by either God or the Devil at any given moment. You can tell by the way they live their life and how they impact people...are they acting in a way that demonstrates the character of God or of the Devil?

The Enemy would love nothing more than to deceive you into believing that everything is God's fault...that God is a mean, unloving, judgmental, joy killer that makes bad things happen to people, but that is the farthest thing from the truth. Please get to know who God and the Devil really are, so that you can make an informed decision. Who is to blame?

In the Bible, names are very important-they explain a person's character. I want you to look at the list below and see the difference between the names of God and the Devil. They both have a lot of names that describe them, but here are just a few.

God	Enemy
Emmanuel=God With Us	Devil=Slanderer
Jehovah Rapha=Healer	Satan=Adversary
Jehovah Jireh=Provider	Father of Lies
Elohim=Creator	Evil One
Yahweh Shalom=Lord of Peace	Tempter
Yahweh=Self-Existent One	Deceiver
I AM=Always Was, Is & Will Be	Accuser of the Brethren

Let's Talk About It

1. What specific memory do you have with God, where you knew it was Him?

_____

_____

_____

_____

_____

2. What do you think the enemy has been lying to you about?

_____

_____

_____

_____

_____

3. Have you been blaming God for something the enemy may have caused?

_____

_____

_____

_____

_____

MICHELLE E. CASWELL   PURELY HIS, INC.

Let's Take Action

Homework

- Look again at the scripture list below and ask the Lord to help you with your unbelief, if you are having a hard time believing that they are true about Him. Really look at who He is and get to know Him for yourself.

- Contact one person. Friendships take effort and real healing happens through accountability.

He is my defender. (Psalm 68:5)

He never gets tired of us. (Isaiah 40:28)

He is my provider. (Philippians 4:19)

He understands everything. (Isaiah 40:28)

He is perfect in every way. (Matthew 5:48)

He is compassionate. (Exodus 34:6)

He doesn't abandon us. (Deuteronomy 31:6)

He is not easily angered. (Exodus 34:6)

He never changes. (Hebrews 13:8)

He is faithful. (Exodus 34:6)

He is perfect love. (1 John 4:8)

He turns bad things into good. (Romans 8:28)

He wants to help us. (Isaiah 41:10)

He is patient. (Psalm 86:15)

He died for me personally. (Romans 5:8)

He is a good Father to everyone. (Ephesians 4:6)

Let's Reflect

What experience did you have with the Lord this week and how were you impacted by it? Where are you still leaving Him out?

_____

_____

_____

_____

_____

_____

_____

_____

_____

_____

_____

_____

_____

_____

_____

_____

_____

MICHELLE E. CASWELL   PURELY HIS, INC.

Week 8-Step 3 Get Unstuck

"So if the Son sets you free, you will be free indeed." John 8:36

Step 3: Get Unstuck (Refer to pages 66-84 in Calling All Workers)

The next several weeks will be spent on Getting Unstuck and this is the crucial step that sets Purely His apart. We are going to assist you in healing from the things that have caused the issues that you are currently struggling with in your life. Whether you have addictions, self-harm issues, anger or marital problems or whatever, all those things come from an unresolved issue in the past (the root cause). It's time to pull out the roots so the symptoms will go away. In Steps 1 & 2, you have all been sharing about your life and pinpointing deep hurts from your past that are presently affecting your life in a negative way.

Now is the time for you to pull out those roots so the symptoms will go away. This is a step that is all about you making a choice. We are going to ask you to choose to surrender, repent and forgive. When you decide to make the choice to change, your life will drastically change.

You have control over your own healing. You can decide to heal in 7 days, 7 weeks, 7 months or 7 years. My encouragement to you is to take a deep breath and ask the Lord to give you Holy courage to make these choices so you can get unstuck.

The Bible says that *"Jesus came to set the captive free"* Isaiah 61:1. My prayer is that you will get free, that you will get unstuck from everything that has held you back from being all that God has called you to be. Take courage and take heart because you are about to get unstuck!

Deal with the Root

*"Get rid of all bitterness, rage and anger, brawling and slander,
along with every form of malice."* Ephesians 4:31

Last week's homework was to review the scripture list about God's character and ask Him to help you with your unbelief. What area are you still struggling to believe about Him?

Now it's time to deal with the root. We all struggle with issues and some of them have been a burden for much of our life. You may have a drug issue, eating disorder, self-harm, promiscuity or anger, but those are not the real issues-they are the symptoms of a deeper issue.

If you want to get rid of these symptoms in your life then you need to look at the root causes and deal with them.

Picture a tree with roots that go very deep and the tree branches are wide and touch and affect several areas of your life. This is also what everyone else sees. If you have unhealthy addictions and ways of acting out, then your branches and leaves lack fruit and look dead. Some of your branches may have fallen on innocent people around you and hurt them. (Nobody sees that the roots of that tree are diseased and therefore there is no way for the branches, leaves and fruit to grow healthy.) It's important to rip out the unhealthy roots to stop the disease from spreading. When the roots are healthy, the tree is healthy and is able to produce good fruit again.

Find the root, pull it out and the symptom goes away. The root can be a lie that you believe to be true, unhealed trauma, an offense, un-confessed sin, a secret, etc. However, a root is generally an unresolved issue. It's important to pay attention and find the original cause of the issue.

No matter how many symptoms you have, there are probably only one or two deep roots that are causing the problem. Look back to a couple of specific incidences in your past that still bother you. If I had the ability to remove one of two of those incidences would your life look completely different now? That incident is most likely the root.

**Getting free is all about choice. It is something we do as a team, with the Lord.
We do our part and He does the rest.**

MICHELLE E. CASWELL   PURELY HIS, INC.

Let's Talk About It

1. What are your thoughts about this concept of root causes and symptoms?

_____

_____

_____

_____

_____

2. What current symptoms do you have?

_____

_____

_____

_____

_____

3. What do you believe the root cause of your symptoms are? Name a specific incident or two.

_____

_____

_____

_____

_____

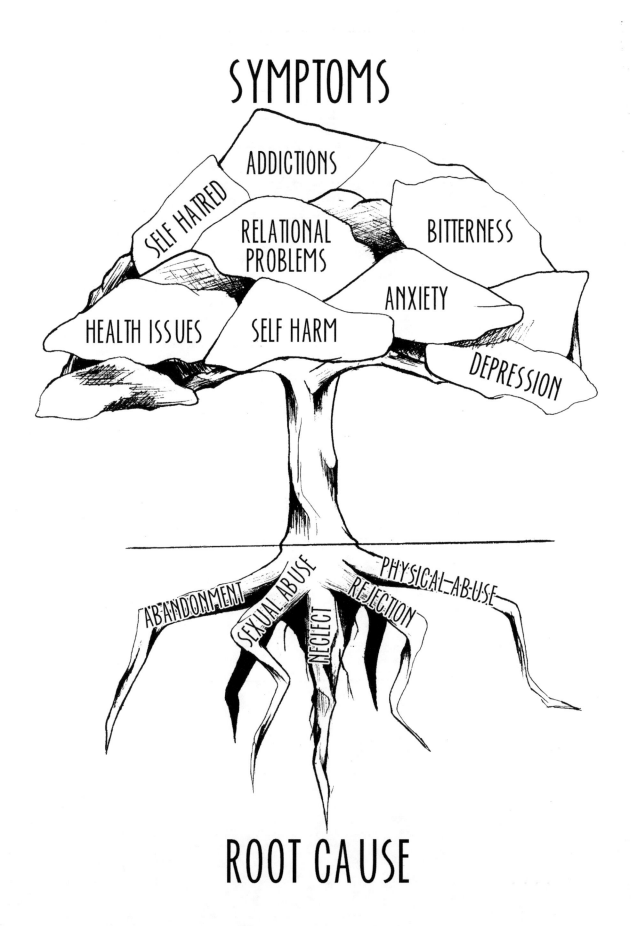

MICHELLE E. CASWELL   PURELY HIS, INC.

Now fill in your symptoms and their roots. Remember that a root is a specific situation.

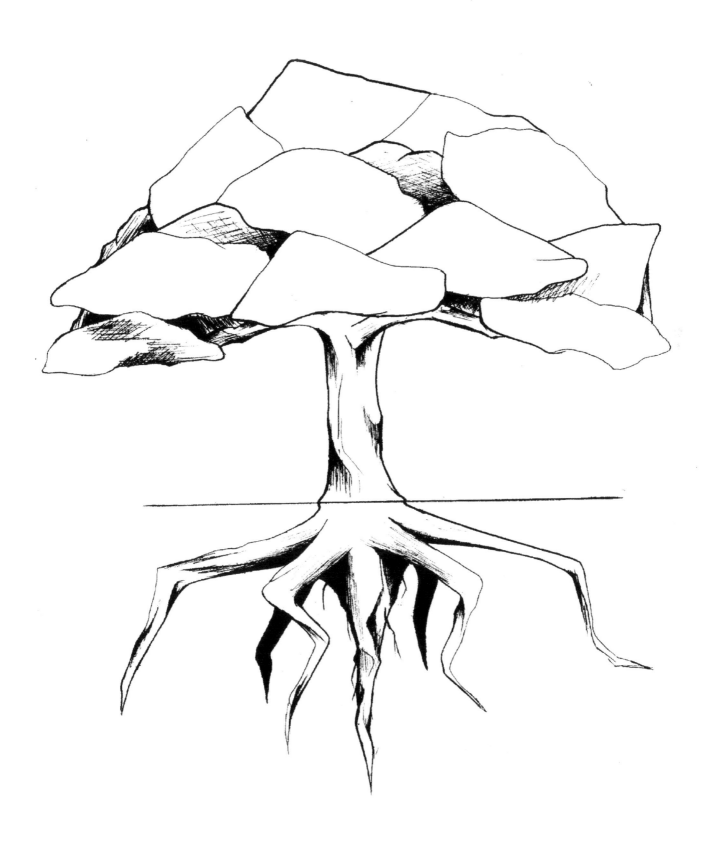

Let's Take Action
Homework

- Begin asking the Lord to give you the courage to look closely at the root causes of your issues and to make some choices to heal from them. Make the choice to walk with Him through this.

- Contact one of your group members and invite them to do something within the next week.

MICHELLE E. CASWELL   PURELY HIS, INC.

Let's Reflect

What are you experiencing after talking about the root causes of your symptoms? What is the Lord showing you?

_____

_____

_____

_____

_____

_____

_____

_____

_____

_____

_____

_____

_____

_____

_____

_____

_____

Week 9 – Receive to Give

"Those who have been forgiven much-love much" (Luke 7:47 paraphrased)

Last week's homework was to ask the Lord to give you the courage to look closely at the root causes of your issues and to make some choices to heal from them. Make the choice to walk with Him through this. How did it go with that?

For the next few weeks we are going to be focusing on forgiveness, which is one of the most effective ways to pull out roots and therefore, Get Unstuck. Forgiveness is the cornerstone of our faith as Christians. Without the cross, without forgiveness, we would have nothing. Forgiveness is the foundation of what we believe, so it is really important to understand the power of it.

The blood of Christ cleanses us from ALL unrighteousness; it sets us free from the punishment of sin and grants us eternal life with God. It allows us the privilege of receiving the person and the power of the Holy Spirit as a comforter and guide through life. We are saved by grace, not by works, so we can't earn it and we don't deserve it. It's a free gift that's offered to everyone; however a lot of people choose not to receive it. It's your choice whether you accept it or not. Sadly, most people choose not accept grace for various reasons. Let's not be one of those people that rejects it.

Receiving forgiveness sets us free and then we're set free on a whole different level when we give away the forgiveness we receive. It's amazing what will take place in your heart when you truly realize what you have been forgiven for. Most people realize what horrible sinners they are when they first choose to receive His forgiveness, but as time goes on…they forget.

If you have lost your joy-the joy you used to have in the beginning…then choosing to receive His forgiveness wholeheartedly again is one of the best ways to get it back. Psalm 51:12 says *"Restore to me the joy of your salvation and grant me a willing spirit, to sustain me."* I truly believe that if you thank the Lord for everything you have been forgiven for or choose to receive forgiveness whole heartedly, then the joy of your salvation will come flooding back in. Today we are going to make the choice to receive forgiveness. Today is the day that you begin to allow forgiveness to change your life.

Feelings of shame, embarrassment, and guilt are indicators of **not receiving** forgiveness and those feelings often keep people from receiving forgiveness. You can also tell if you haven't received His forgiveness if you keep asking for it, over and over again for the same thing that is in your past. Receiving forgiveness has the ability to set you free from those uncomfortable feelings. Forgiveness is a choice to receive and to give. But you can't give away, what you don't possess. You can't give love if you haven't received it and you can't forgive unless you have been forgiven.

Some sins are going to be easy for you to ask for and receive forgiveness. But there are other sins…sins that have caused a lot of heartache that aren't as easy to receive forgiveness for. Those are the ones you really need to clear up with God, because as you know…the pain inside is intense and it's still affecting you. Here's the good news, if you are a Christian then you have been forgiven of EVERY sin that you have committed and ever will commit, that's the truth. Your only responsibility this week is to **receive it**-God has already done the rest!

When He had received the drink, Jesus said, "It is finished." With that, He bowed His head and gave up His spirit. John 19:30

MICHELLE E. CASWELL   PURELY HIS, INC.

Let's Talk About It

1. Is this a different understanding of forgiveness than you are used to?

_____

_____

_____

2. Do you believe that you have received forgiveness for everything? Is there something that you keep asking forgiveness for over and over again?

_____

_____

_____

3. Why is it hard for you to receive forgiveness?

_____

_____

_____

Let's pray this out. If you believe that you have received all of God's forgiveness then take this opportunity to thank Him for all that you have been forgiven for. It will restore the joy of your salvation. If there is something you aren't sure you've been forgiven for, then ask for forgiveness <u>one more time</u> and actually **receive** it this time.

It will go something like "Lord, thank you for making the choice to forgive me for everything I've <u>ever</u> done wrong and <u>ever</u> will do. Thank you for forgiving me for (be specific) _____, _____, _____. Thank you that what you did on the cross for me was sufficient. You said "It is finished." Lord, I **receive** your forgiveness and I'm done playing God in my own life, deciding whether <u>I deserve</u> forgiveness or not. Thank you Lord."

Next week you'll be giving away the forgiveness that you received today.

Let's Take Action

Homework

- Write a list of the things you are thankful to have been forgiven for, so you don't forget.
- Contact someone and encourage them with a scripture this week, whether by text, email or a phone call.

Thank you Lord for forgiving me for:

_____

_____

_____

_____

_____

_____

Who did you call and what scripture did you give them?

_____

_____

_____

_____

_____

_____

_____

MICHELLE E. CASWELL   PURELY HIS, INC.

Let's Reflect

What are you feeling after talking about these things?
What is the Lord showing you about forgiveness?

_____

_____

_____

_____

_____

_____

_____

_____

_____

_____

_____

_____

_____

_____

_____

_____

_____

_____

_____

Week 10 – Forgiving Others

"Forgive as I have forgiven you" (Colossians 3:13)

Last week's homework was to write a list of the things you are thankful to have been forgiven for, so you don't forget. Did that help you feel more grateful for what Jesus really did for you?

We have all heard someone say, *"I've already forgiven that person."* However, their face tells you a different story. They are still bitter. I think they believe that they have forgiven because they said the "words," but I believe they have a misunderstanding of forgiveness and how to effectively forgive.

When you choose to forgive, you are forgiving a debt owed against you. You are choosing not to hold that debt against them and you don't expect them to pay you back for the wrong. Instead, you are choosing to make them owe God instead of you. Forgiveness is a choice, not a feeling and choosing to give away forgiveness will bring incredible freedom to you. In fact, the obedience of forgiving others pleases God, because it shows Him that we love Him by doing what He asks. *"If you love Me, you will keep My commandments."* John 14:15

Another good reason to forgive others is that holding un-forgiveness is considered un-repented sin, which gives Satan permission to camp there and torment you. Choosing to forgive others, takes care of that sin and makes the enemy flee-he will no longer have permission to hold onto that area.

Once you have received forgiveness then it is your responsibility to forgive others. When someone hurts you (whether they meant to or not), they offended you. Forgiving the offense will remove the root of bitterness, which is often referred to as the "Cancer to the soul" because it eats away at you and causes all kinds of other problems. But don't worry, if bitterness has already taken root, then forgiveness is how you pull it out.

Forgiveness is not a feeling, it's an action. You will never FEEL like forgiving someone who has wronged you and you will definitely never FEEL like forgiving yourself. But you really need to. It will set you free in so many ways. The Lord does not distinguish between which sins we should forgive and which ones we shouldn't. He doesn't say, "Take your sweet time forgiving." He just says to *DO IT*.

Forgiveness doesn't mean that "it" never happened, nor does it excuse the bad behavior of another or imply that the offense wasn't wrong. Forgiveness is not between you and the other person, it's between you and God. By forgiving, you will choose to not allow that person's actions to abuse you, hurt you or hold you in bondage anymore.

When someone hurts you and you don't forgive them right away, it's as if that person and that incident are hooked onto you and you are dragging them through life with you. Think of all the people hooked to your back right now through un-forgiveness. Aren't they getting heavy? That is the spot where you are stuck. You are stuck in the past and it is still affecting you today.

Picture this: In prayer, you choose to unhook them (and what they did to you) from you and hook them to God. By doing that, you are removing your record of wrongs against them and are free to move on without all the weight. You are also saying *"You don't owe me anymore. You owe God."*

Over the next few weeks you are going to forgive <u>everyone</u> that you have something against. My suggestion for your future is: when new hurts happen (and they will) forgive quickly.

You are going to love how you feel after you forgive. Warning; it doesn't feel good during, but it feels good afterwards. You will get through it. The enemy will try to confuse and convince you that you didn't really mean it and suggest that, *"If you meant it, then why are you still hurt over it?"* You may still have hurt feelings for a short time, but God will heal those too, **if** you surrender them to Him.

Here is an example of how to pray a prayer of forgiveness.

Lord, thank you so much for forgiving me for everything. Thank you for forgiving me for (be specific). I know I don't deserve Your forgiveness, but You gave it to me anyways and Lord I receive it right now. When I remind myself of what I have been forgiven for, it makes it easier for me to forgive others. I know that You command me to forgive those that have hurt me and forgive others as You have forgiven me...so that's what I'm going to do right now. Lord, I choose to forgive _____ (Use their name) for _____ and _____ (be specific). That day changed my life and hurt me so deeply, and it continues to hurt me now. So Lord, I am unhooking _____ (person's name) from me and I am hooking him/her to you. He/she no longer owes me anything. He/she owes you now. And Lord I ask that you heal me from the hurt that their choice caused me. I don't want to hurt anymore and I don't want that part of my past to continue robbing me of what you have for me in the present.

(This following part can be very difficult, but I believe you can do it. You are going to get unstuck and experience the freedom that the Lord has waiting for you.)

Lord, I also want to pray for him/her...that you would bless him/her and help him/her find you and I pray that they will give their life to you. Have mercy on their soul...Amen.

Let's Talk About It

1. What situation have you been holding against God?

_____

_____

_____

_____

2. What reasons would make you not want to forgive others?

_____

_____

_____

_____

3. Have you ever thought of forgiveness as a form of spiritual battle? What do you think about that?

_____

_____

_____

_____

Let's pray it out together.

Points to remember:

*   Pray out-loud so Satan can hear you.
*   Forgive the specifics.
*   Forgive from your perspective even if it might not be accurate.
*   Don't excuse other's behavior.
*   Be direct not passive.
*   Pay attention to pictures or words in your head.
*   Go slow and listen to the Lord.

Let's Take Action

Homework

- Journal: What is the Lord showing you about the things you have been holding onto and how it has been affecting you?

- Contact someone from the group and share one thing you have realized about forgiveness.

MICHELLE E. CASWELL   PURELY HIS, INC.

Let's Reflect

What is the Lord showing you about the things you have been holding onto
and how it has been affecting you?

_____

_____

_____

_____

_____

_____

_____

_____

_____

_____

_____

_____

_____

_____

_____

_____

_____

_____

Week 11 – Forgiving Yourself

"Therefore, there is now no condemnation for those who are in Christ Jesus, because through Christ Jesus, the law of the Spirit who gives life, has set you free from the law of sin and death." Romans 8:1-2

Last week's homework was to journal about what the Lord has been showing you about the things you have been holding onto. How have those things been affecting you?

Today we're going to talk about the blessings and difficulties in forgiving yourself. It took a lot of forgiving of others to obtain the freedom I now have, but forgiving myself was the most difficult by far. I believe it's because I hold myself to a much higher standard than I hold others to or maybe I don't like to admit that I'm wrong. Are you the same way?

The thing that helped me finally make the choice to forgive myself, was that I realized it was necessary for me to heal. The Lord revealed that I was being arrogant by not forgiving myself, because He already forgave me. Was I smarter than God? Was I putting myself above Him?

Forgiving yourself is making the choice to unhook your sin from yourself and hook it to God. He then takes it, rolls it up into a ball and chucks it into the sea of forgetfulness, never to be brought up again. Micah 7:19

We all have reasons for why we don't want to forgive ourselves. We think:

- I have done terrible things that still affect people today.
- I knew better and did it anyways.
- I continue to do the same thing over and over.
- They haven't forgiven me so I can't forgive myself.
- I don't deserve it.

Although, those are really good reasons and probably true...you cannot use them as excuses. None of these reasons are good enough...it's time to get free from all that condemnation you've been living under. You signed up for this group so you could learn how to go ALL in with Jesus and get UNSTUCK from **anything** in the way of that. Well...this is how you do just that. I believe that this week is going to be a pivotal moment in your healing journey, because forgiving myself set me free probably more than any other choice I made and I believe it's going to be just as powerful for you.

Let's Talk About It

1. What is going to be the hardest thing to forgive yourself for?

_____

_____

_____

_____

_____

2. What is the reason you have not forgiven yourself yet?

_____

_____

_____

_____

_____

3. You may not **feel** like it, but are you **ready** to make the choice to forgive yourself now?

_____

_____

_____

_____

_____

Let's Pray It Out

Let's Take Action

Homework

- Journal about the freedom you have been experiencing from choosing to forgive.

- Contact someone in the group that you haven't yet or that you don't contact very often. Start to step out of your comfort zone.

Let's Reflect

What are you feeling after sharing these things?
How have you been feeling after you forgive someone?

_____

_____

_____

_____

_____

_____

_____

_____

_____

_____

_____

_____

_____

_____

_____

_____

_____

MICHELLE E. CASWELL   PURELY HIS, INC.

Week 12 – Forgiving God & Everyone Else

*"And when you stand praying, if you hold **anything** against **anyone**, forgive them, so that your Father in heaven may forgive your sins." Mark 11:25*

Last week's homework was to journal about the freedom that you have been experiencing from choosing to forgive. Tell us about that freedom.

Sometimes there is some residual stuff that comes up, like one or two memories that keep resurfacing. That doesn't mean you didn't forgive that person, it just means you need to forgive them for something specific. It's forgiving them from another angle.

When we are praying to forgive someone else, there is a tendency for the Lord to bring to your memory a person or situation that you forgot all about. When that happens, just pray it out. You have been learning how to forgive alongside those in your group, but you are also learning how to do this on your own. When it comes to the big ones, you will probably still want to find a prayer partner to pray it out together. But eventually you will be doing the smaller ones on your own.

When forgiving others, think about all the people in your life that have affected you in a negative way. Don't let them have power over you anymore...unhook them! Here is a list of people you may have forgotten about:

- Bullies
- Coworkers or Bosses
- Teachers
- Friends
- Landlords
- Ex-lovers
- Church Leadership
- God

When you choose to forgive those that have hurt you, including God, the symptoms of bitterness will go away and Satan will have nothing to hold onto. I have been told a few times that it is wrong or sacrilegious to forgive God, but I disagree. He is a relational God and it's hard to have a healthy relationship with someone if you have something against them, because you will harbor distrust. Besides, God is not surprised that you have something against Him. He knows you do and He wants it out of the way so that you can develop a healthy relationship with Him.

I find it ironic that most people do not blame Satan (the Deceiver) for things that have happened to them or others, instead they blame God. I know I did. We say things like, *"God could have stopped it from happening, if He wanted."*

What about man's free will? What about Satan's free will? Let's all try and keep those questions in our mind when accusing God of injustice in the future.

However, when it comes to forgiving God or anyone else, it needs to be done from your perspective, whether it is accurate or not. An example would be: *"Lord, I forgive you for making my mom cheat on my dad and ruining my life. Lord, I also forgive you for turning your back on me and abandoning me when I needed you most."* It doesn't matter whether it's the truth or not-it's my truth. It's important to forgive from your perspective, because that is exactly what you are holding against God or that person.

Even though it might not sound right to forgive a perfect God, forgiveness is necessary to trust and rely on Him in the future. He wants a relationship with you. He forgave you. Don't you think it's time you forgave Him? Wouldn't it be awesome to have a "do over" with the Lord and have a "clean slate?"

The Lord tells us to forgive others as we have been forgiven and He would never tell us to do something that He hasn't given us the power to pull off.

Let's Talk About It

1. Who or what has been brought to your mind that you had forgotten all about?

_____

_____

_____

_____

_____

2. Is there someone that you know you need to forgive, but you feel like you can't?

_____

_____

_____

_____

_____

3. Can you see how making forgiveness a lifestyle is a healthy choice?

_____

_____

_____

_____

_____

Let's Take Action

Homework

- Forgive someone on your own this week. Be ready to tell us about it next week. Make sure you do it out loud.

- Contact someone just to encourage them.

MICHELLE E. CASWELL   PURELY HIS, INC.

Let's Reflect

What are you feeling about these things? Who did you forgive and how did it go?

_____

_____

_____

_____

_____

_____

_____

_____

_____

_____

_____

_____

_____

_____

_____

_____

_____

Week 13 – All In

*"But seek **first** His kingdom and His righteousness, and all these things will be given to you as well."* Matthew 6:33

Last week you were supposed to forgive someone on your own. How did that go?

You may have given your heart to Jesus, but have you ever given your whole life to Him? Call it surrender, call it rededicating your life, but when you truly decide to go ALL in...your life will never be the same. The goal of Purely His is for you to choose to go ALL in with Jesus. And you are literally one choice away from that. Someone who is ALL in becomes an on-fire Christian whose life impacts everyone around them. This is what you've been waiting for-this is where you go from cold or luke-warm to HOT.

This is where you decide:

- "Not my will, but Yours, Lord" to put your whole life in His hands: past, present and future. "I'm done doing life on my own. I want and need Your help, so here You go. Here's my life."

- To surrender your worry and any anxious thoughts that concern you. Worrying is a lack of trust in the Lord.

- To give Him all your mistakes, sins and even future dreams to Him.

- To place your whole life in His hands every day.

- To live a repentant life for Him.

- To make Jesus your #1 priority-your first love.

- To no longer conform to the ways of the world.

Surrendering your life to the Lord is an action of trust, not a feeling. However, when you live out the action first-the feeling will follow.

Let's Talk About It

1. Does going 'all in with Jesus' scare you? If so, why?

_____

_____

_____

_____

_____

2. What have you been holding onto...that the Lord is asking you to let go of?

_____

_____

_____

_____

_____

3. Are you ready to go ALL IN?

_____

_____

_____

_____

Let's pray it out together right now!

MICHELLE E. CASWELL   PURELY HIS, INC.

Let's Take Action

Homework

- Journal. How is your life going to look different after making this decision?
- Contact one of your fellow group members and share a prayer request you have and ask if you can pray for their situation.

Let's Reflect

What will your life look like after making the decision to go all in?

_____

_____

_____

_____

_____

_____

_____

_____

_____

_____

_____

_____

_____

_____

_____

_____

_____

_____

MICHELLE E. CASWELL   PURELY HIS, INC.

Week 14 – Confession

"Confess your sins one to another. Pray for one another and
you shall be healed" James 5:16

Last week's homework was to journal how your life will be different after making the decision to 'go all in with Jesus.' Tell us about one thing that will be different.

Isn't that scripture an amazing promise? I don't know about you, but I can always use some more healing.

Confession is a natural process that usually doesn't need much prompting when you are in close relationship with people. This is especially true when you've decided to grow in the Lord together, like all of you have. It's easy to recognize a confession because someone will say, *"I can't believe I'm sharing this with you"* or *"I've never told anyone about this"*.

When things are kept in the dark (secret), the enemy can torment us. The enemy makes us feel ashamed, guilty or afraid. Confession brings the dark secret into the light where Jesus can heal it.

Confession is usually a relief to the person who has been holding onto it, because the secret loses its power as soon as it is exposed. Don't be surprised when you get "buyer's remorse" right after you confess a sin or secret struggle. You may think something like, *"I wish I wouldn't have said so much"*. It is totally normal to have "buyer's remorse". To help ease the discomfort, encourage each other by proclaiming that you are not judging anyone.

This should become a regular part of your Christian walk. Find a couple of people that you can confess things to on a regular basis. These people should know your struggles and hold you accountable. This will keep you on the path of righteousness.

Let's Talk About It

1. What holds you back from telling people your secret(s)?

_____

_____

_____

_____

_____

2. What have you been set free from since we started? Keeping in mind that we only have a short time left, what do you want to still get free from?

_____

_____

_____

_____

_____

3. Do you have anything that is hidden that needs to come to the light and be healed?

_____

_____

_____

_____

MICHELLE E. CASWELL   PURELY HIS, INC.

Let's Take Action

Homework

- Choose a couple of people of the same gender (unless you are struggling with same sex attraction) that could be on your accountability team.

- Call them and ask them to be on that team.

Let's Reflect

What are you feeling after sharing these things? Who did you choose
to be on your accountability team and why?

_____

_____

_____

_____

_____

_____

_____

_____

_____

_____

_____

_____

_____

_____

_____

_____

_____

MICHELLE E. CASWELL   PURELY HIS, INC.

Week 15 – Repentance is Love

"Repent, for the kingdom of heaven has come near." Matthew 3:2

Last week's homework was to choose an accountability team. Who did you choose?

Purely His is an End Time's ministry, because we believe that Jesus is coming back soon and we need to be ready and help others get ready. Wouldn't it be awesome to be able to run to Him when He comes back instead of shrinking back in shame because of how you are living?

Love is an action, not just a feeling. We show God that we love Him by being obedient and doing what He says. The main thing God is asking us to do is to love Him and love others.

One of the greatest ways to love the Lord is through living a repented life. Repentance is turning away from sin and turning towards the Lord. It is another form of surrendering: you are choosing to surrender your sinful lifestyle, in exchange for living the way the Lord desires.

Once you make the decision to repent, you need to walk out that decision. The Bible says that we are to: *"Produce fruit in keeping with repentance"* Luke 3:8. Your life should start looking different after making the choice to repent.

To make this process a little easier, focus on the Lord instead of the sin you are trying not to return to. If a drug addict wants to quit drugs they shouldn't constantly look at the drugs and say to themselves, *"Try not to think about drugs. Don't think about drugs,"* since that makes them focus on it all the more. It's much easier to take your eyes off the sin and focus on Jesus instead. The closer we get to Him, the further we move away from sin.

Picture the Lord coming back right at this second. Is there anything that you are involved in that you would be ashamed of? If the answer is yes, then that is what you need to repent of.

Let's Talk About It

1. What just came to your mind that you need to repent from?

_____

_____

_____

_____

2. Are you afraid to repent from that and why?

_____

_____

_____

_____

3. What will repentance look like for you?

_____

_____

_____

_____

MICHELLE E. CASWELL   PURELY HIS, INC.

Let's Take Action

Homework

- Journal: What will repentance look like for you?
- Call or visit someone in person and pray for them out loud.

Let's Reflect

How are you feeling after sharing these things? What is the Lord showing you about your sin and why you need to repent?

_____

_____

_____

_____

_____

_____

_____

_____

_____

_____

_____

_____

_____

_____

_____

_____

_____

MICHELLE E. CASWELL   PURELY HIS, INC.

Week 16-Taking Ground Back

"The thief comes only to steal and kill and destroy; I have come that
they may have life, and have it to the full." John 10:10

Last week you were supposed to journal what repentance would look like for you. How did you answer that question?

When I was two years into my healing the Lord said to me, "Michelle, I'm giving you back everything that Satan stole from you, EVERYTHING!"

I didn't realize that Satan had stolen from me. Maybe you can relate? I always blamed myself and other people for all the hard times I endured, but there was an evil force working behind the scenes to kill, steal and destroy me and he used every possible means to do just that.

Satan took so much from me: the security of growing up in a two parent home, my innocence, my sound mind, my marriages, the list goes on and on. Instead of sitting back and letting him take any more from us, how about we choose to reclaim what belongs to the Lord and take ground back from the Enemy, because he has stolen what is not his.

Proverbs 6 says, *"Excuses might be found for a thief who steals because he is starving. But if he is caught, he must pay back seven times what he stole, even if he has to sell everything in his house."*

How would you like to get back seven times what has been stolen from you? Can you imagine what that would look like?

Let's CHOOSE to take back our families, our dreams, our sound minds, our marriages, our self-worth, our dignity, our friendships, and everything else the Enemy has stolen!

Knowing scripture about who you are in Christ and the authority you possess is extremely important when you are attempting to take back ground from the Enemy. Read these truths and ask the Lord to seal them in your heart, so you will have them when you need them.

- *"You, dear children, are from God and have overcome them, because the one who is in you is greater than the one who is in the world." 1 John 4:4*

- *"Submit yourselves, then, to God. Resist the devil, and he will flee from you."* James 4:7

- *"They triumphed over him by the blood of the Lamb and by the word of their testimony; they did not love their lives so much as to shrink from death."* Revelation 12:11

Let's Talk About It

1. What has Satan stolen from you?

_____

_____

_____

2. Do you believe it is possible to get back what was stolen?

_____

_____

_____

3. Satan is the Deceiver and the Father of Lies. How has he lied to you?

_____

_____

_____

Here is an example of how I have prayed to 'Take Ground Back.' Keep in mind that this type of prayer is intense, so do not be passive about it. <u>Take it by force!</u>

"Lord Jesus, I thank you that I belong to You. I just realized that Satan has been stealing from me and I have the ability in Your name, to demand those things be given back. I ask you Lord to protect and guide me as I stand up to the Enemy.

Satan, I proclaim to you that I belong to the Lord Jesus Christ and you must return everything that you stole from me. The Lord rebuke you! I command you to return all that you stole and I take authority in Jesus mighty name over my _____, _____, _____, _____,_____ (my children, my friends, my husband, my sister, my parents, my life, my job, my emotions, my health, etc.) and I commit them all to the Lord for His honor and glory. Any and all agreements I made with you, knowingly or unknowingly, I now break off in the name of Jesus Christ. You don't own me. Jesus owns me. I was bought with a price and I belong to Him.

Lord, Jesus please open my eyes to the creative ways you are going to redeem everything Satan stole (innocence, childhood, relationships, etc.). I know that it may not be in the exact form it was taken, but I trust that you have a good plan for all of this. In Jesus' name, Amen."

MICHELLE E. CASWELL   PURELY HIS, INC.

Let's Take Action

Homework

- Write a list of the things Satan has stolen from you and then we are going to pray it out and demand that he give it back. We are going to take authority over those things again and then surrender them to the Lord.
- Contact someone from your group.

Things that Satan stole from me:

_____

_____

_____

_____

_____

_____

_____

_____

_____

_____

_____

_____

_____

_____

_____

_____

Let's Reflect

What are you feeling or experiencing after talking about these things? What do you think about the power you have to reclaim what has been stolen?

_____

_____

_____

_____

_____

_____

_____

_____

_____

_____

_____

_____

_____

_____

_____

_____

_____

MICHELLE E. CASWELL   PURELY HIS, INC.

Week 17-Step 4 Walk It Out

"As a prisoner for the Lord, then, I urge you to live a life
worthy of the calling you have received." Ephesians 4:1

Step 4: Walk It Out (Refer to pages 84-92 in Calling All Workers)

The next few weeks will be spent learning how to 'Walk It Out.' By this time you have learned a lot of truths about God, yourself, and those around you. Now you need to start taking those truths from head knowledge to heart knowledge. It's time to make it your reality, by walking out what you say you believe. This is a 'faith in action' step. It's not enough to just know stuff in your head-you need to practice what you preach and live in a manner that shows your life has changed.

It's important that you start living out what you say you believe. If you say you believe the Bible, then let your life reflect that. Walk it out! It's important that you really take to heart what He says. If you say that the Bible is true and God is not a liar then you also know that God has spoken some awesome truths and promises over you.

He says, *"With man this is impossible, but with God **all** things are possible,"* if you believe that, then walk it out. The Bible also says, *"I can do all things through Christ Jesus who strengthens me."* If you believe that, then walk it out. If you believe that God said, *"Do not fear or do not be anxious for anything,"* then walk it out. Are you getting the picture?

This is the season where we are going to strongly encourage you to start walking out what you say you believe. So get ready to be challenged, and to grow even more than you already have. This whole thing we do with Jesus, this race that we are running, starts with a walk. Are you ready?

Start Walking

"Be doers of the word and not just hearers only, deceiving yourselves" James 1:22

There are enough phonies in the world today, even in the church. Let's not be one of them. Let's choose to actually walk out what we say we believe. It's time to live out what you have been learning about yourself and the Lord. You have made some choices about how you're going to live, so let's choose to walk out those decisions together. You have decided to go all in with Jesus, you've surrendered a bunch of things, you've repented, and you've forgiven.

This is where you really need to begin challenging one another to proclaim who you are and what you stand for. It may get a little confrontational, especially when someone isn't living the way they said they were going to. Confrontation is a good thing though...the Bible says *"Preach the word; be prepared in season and out of season; correct,* **rebuke** *and encourage--with great patience and careful instruction"* 2 Timothy 4:2. If someone said in your presence that they made a decision to change this or that, then you have the right to "call them out" especially in the context of your group.

Here are some practical ways to 'Walk it Out.' One way is by going on a prayer walk and therefore, change your thinking, emotions and habits at the same time. A prayer walk is where you walk and pray out loud with a purpose. This can be done one-on-one, in a group or alone. It doesn't even have to be a real "walk"...it can happen while someone is alone in the shower, the car, while cooking, cleaning, or journaling.

Praise Walk: When you are down and need a pick-me-up or are anxious and haven't felt the presence of the Lord in a while, then try a *Praise Walk*. Learn to praise Him in everything—especially when things aren't going the way you want them to. This is where everything that you pray is a praise. *"Lord I thank you for my salvation, my family, the sun, my job, etc."* It blesses the Lord's heart when you appreciate what He has done and is doing for you.

Surrender Walk: A good walk for those times where the burdens feel very heavy. Jesus told us, *"Come all you who are weary and heavily burdened and I will give you rest"* (Matthew 11:28). From the little stuff to the big stuff, give it to Him through prayer until you feel the relief of the burden being lifted. *"Lord I give you my fear right now, my family, my bills, my friend's personal problems."*

Intercessory Walk: This is an excellent walk for those that are self-centered, depressed or worried about others. Focusing on others in prayer will make you feel better-the more you focus on others, the happier you will be. We are to become more like Jesus. *"Christ Jesus who died--more than that, who was raised to life--is at the right hand of God and is also* **interceding** *for us"* Romans 8:24

MICHELLE E. CASWELL   PURELY HIS, INC.

Let's Talk About It

1. What new truths have you learned about yourself that you are willing to walk out now?

_____

_____

_____

_____

_____

2. What are some ways you could do that this week? Make it personal.

_____

_____

_____

_____

_____

3. Which one of these prayer walks will be most helpful to you?

_____

_____

_____

_____

_____

Let's Take Action

Homework

- Go on a Prayer Walk with someone from your group. Do not chit chat with each other during your walk, but rather pray. Take turns speaking to the Lord as you give Him anything and everything you can think of.
- Journal your praises, by creating a praise list. This works great when you are anxious, can't feel God, or you're feeling discontented.
- Brainstorm ideas for service project. Next week planning

Write a list of praises, things to surrender and people to intercede for.

Thank you Lord for:

_____

_____

_____

Lord I give you:

_____

_____

_____

Lord I pray for:

_____

_____

_____

MICHELLE E. CASWELL   PURELY HIS, INC.

Let's Reflect

What are you feeling or experiencing after taking this approach to prayer?

_____

_____

_____

_____

_____

_____

_____

_____

_____

_____

_____

_____

_____

_____

_____

_____

_____

_____

Week 18 –Joy in Serving

"Jesus came to serve, not be served." Matthew 20:28

Last week you were supposed to go on a Prayer Walk. Tell us about your experience with that.

Jesus left us with an amazing example of how we should live to serve God and others with our lives. There is such joy in serving someone else. The Lord says "love God and love people" (Matthew 22:36-39) and serving is a great way to do just that. We are simply following Jesus and His example.

Most of us like to think of ourselves as being a good servant, but the true test is when someone treats you like a servant. How do you respond? Does it bother you when someone bosses you around or treats you as less than or doesn't give you the credit you think you deserve? It's amazing how we respond to those things.

When I was in rehab we had jobs that we did to help pay for the program we were in. One of those jobs was cleaning a church. I remember the rehab director Monica gave me a set of keys and told me, *"Clip it to your belt loop."* I sarcastically responded, *"What am I...a janitor?"*

She quickly responded with, *"God set you free from a horrific lifestyle and this is the thanks you give Him? You outta be thankful that He is allowing you to clean the floors of this church."*

Her response to my complaint immediately put me in my place. Who did I think I was? I had so much arrogance, so much pride and I needed to humble myself. In James 4:10 it says *"Humble yourselves before the Lord, and He will lift you up."*

I am happy to report that I am pretty good at serving now and it has become a real joy to serve others and not get anything out of it, other than knowing that I am a blessing to the Lord and His people.

This week your group is going to plan a service project together. It will allow you to use your gifts, walk out your new faith, learn to live a selfless life and become more like Jesus in the process. This is also a great way for you to build strong well-rounded relationships between those in your group. You have been healing together, learning together and now you're going to serve together.

Let's Talk About It

1. When you think about being a servant...do you like that idea or do you despise the thought? Keep it real.

   _____

   _____

   _____

   _____

   _____

2. Thinking about the different gifts and hearts we all have, what could you do with your God given gifts to love this world?

   _____

   _____

   _____

   _____

3. Who could we serve together next week? Let's toss around some ideas and plan something.

   _____

   _____

   _____

   _____

MICHELLE E. CASWELL   PURELY HIS, INC.

Let's Take Action

Service Project

_____

Date, Time & Location

_____

Project manager

_____

Who are we serving?

_____

_____

What are we doing?

_____

_____

What is the heart behind this project?

Supplies needed:

To-Do list:

Jobs:

Homework

- Pray for the service project that the Lord would change a life through it, even if the life is yours.
- Contact someone from your group.

Let's Reflect

What are you feeling after talking about these things? What is the Lord showing you about your view of being a servant?

_____

_____

_____

_____

_____

_____

_____

_____

_____

_____

_____

_____

_____

_____

_____

_____

MICHELLE E. CASWELL   PURELY HIS, INC.

Week 19 – Love

"Teacher, which is the greatest commandment in the Law?" Jesus replied: "'Love the Lord your God with all your heart and with all your soul and with all your mind.' This is the first and greatest commandment. And the second is like it: 'Love your neighbor as yourself." Matthew 22:36-40

Last week your group started planning the service project. How are the plans going?

This week we're going to talk about love, which can be a hard topic for some people. I know it was for me, because I thought I was broken in that area. I had messed up countless times concerning love and didn't feel very good at it. I also did not believe that I was loveable or worthy of love.

I knew I needed to *"get good"* at love though, because it is the most important character quality to possess as a Christian. Most people try to do it apart from God and wonder why their relationships keep failing. The reason is that you can't truly love without the Holy Spirit moving freely through you. Loving others is something we do WITH the Lord not FOR Him.

Take heart because God is love. He created you in His image and He is in you, so He will teach you how to love. He will even love others through you if you let Him. Keep in mind that you can't give what you don't have. Since the Lord has offered you His great love, CHOOSE to receive it.

Love is an action, not just a feeling. Learn to have the action and watch the feelings follow.

Read the following scriptures for the Biblical definition of love.

Love is:

Love is patient, love is kind. It does not envy, it does not boast, it is not proud. It does not dishonor others, it is not self-seeking, it is not easily angered, it keeps no record of wrongs. Love does not delight in evil but rejoices with the truth. It always protects, always trusts, always hopes, it always perseveres. Love never fails. 1 Corinthians 13:4-8

The Bible says that God is love, so I inserted His name below:

God is patient, God is kind. He does not envy, He does not boast, He is not proud. God does not dishonor others, He is not self-seeking, God is not easily angered, He keeps no record of wrongs. God does not delight in evil but rejoices with the truth. God always protects, always trusts, always hopes, He always perseveres. God never fails. 1 Corinthians 13:4-8

Now I want you to insert your name in the place of love.

I am:

_____ is patient, _____ is kind. _____ does not envy, _____ does not boast, _____ is not proud. _____ does not dishonor others, _____ is not self-seeking, _____ is not easily angered, _____ keeps no record of wrongs. _____ does not delight in evil but rejoices with the truth. _____ always protects, always trusts, always hopes, always perseveres _____ never fails.

MICHELLE E. CASWELL   PURELY HIS, INC.

Let's Talk About It

1. When you saw your name written within the scripture, which word did not describe your current personality at all?

_____

_____

_____

_____

_____

2. Have you received the love of God or is something preventing you?

_____

_____

_____

_____

_____

3. Do you have some work to do in the area of love?

_____

_____

_____

_____

_____

Let's Take Action

Homework

- Focus on loving people in action-then journal about it.
- Contact someone from your group this week and show them some love. Get creative.

MICHELLE E. CASWELL   PURELY HIS, INC.

Let's Reflect

What are you experiencing after talking about these things? How did you express the action of love this week?

_____

_____

_____

_____

_____

_____

_____

_____

_____

_____

_____

_____

_____

_____

_____

_____

_____

_____

_____

Week 20-Step 5 Take Someone with You

*"First take the plank out of your own eye, **and then** you will see clearly to remove the speck from your brother's eye."* Matthew 7:5

Last week you were supposed to focus on loving people in action and then journaling about it. How did that go?

Step 5: Take Someone with You (Refer to pages 92-95 in Calling All Workers)

I am so excited about this step! This is one of my absolute favorite things to do and I hope it becomes your favorite thing as well. Watching your life change is a miracle in itself, but then watching how you are able to lead somebody else into that same kind of freedom is where you hit the jackpot.

When it comes to 'taking someone with you', it starts with looking at those around you and saying *"Hey! I'm already following Christ, so follow me as I follow Christ."* That is discipleship/mentoring. That is 'taking someone with you'. It's living life transparently alongside each other.

You didn't go through everything for nothing. God has a purpose for all of it. This is the step where 'your story' gets used to help another person the way you have been helped. This is where it really counts. This is where 'your story' has the possibility of changing the lives of those you mentor.

You have received healing, freedom, encouragement, hope and comfort and those things can now be used to help others. The truths that were used to set you free, can set others free as well, so don't keep them to yourself.

You only need to be one step ahead of someone to take them by the hand and invite them on the journey with you. The Bible talks about "first removing the log out of your eye so that you can remove the sliver out of another's eye." So as you get free from different things-just watch! As soon as you get free from something, all of a sudden God will bring someone to you that is stuck in that same area. You will know how to get them unstuck because you just got unstuck yourself.

I want to encourage you to make 'taking someone with you' a lifestyle. Never, ever stop learning and growing and allowing God to use you SO THAT you can help others do the same. This is where life begins to have incredible purpose: when we are helping others have the freedom we are now experiencing.

Called To Disciple

*"Go into **all** the world and make disciples of all men" Matthew 28: 19*

Last week you were supposed to focus on loving people in action and then journal about it. How did you do with that?

The Lord has a heart for the whole world to be saved and He wants to partner with us to accomplish that. Think about it, we all have a circle of influence and God has also given us a unique heart for different people so we can reach the world for Him. All of our past experiences, once surrendered and healed, have the power to heal others and bring them into this new life of freedom with the Lord.

I know that some of you are intimidated by the thought of mentoring others, but here's the exciting news; you've already been actively mentoring in this group. Every time you shared your story, gave advice, prayed for someone, shared your past failures and your future dreams...you were 'taking someone with you.' You were mentoring. Plus the people in your life outside of this group have also witnessed your transformation which is another form of mentoring.

The Lord will continue to use your life to attract others to Himself...to seek Him and the healing He offers. He wants to use you and has full confidence in His abilities to change the world through you. 'Taking others with you' is a tremendous blessing. Watching lives change, seeing marriages restored, watching people get free from addictions and seeing hopes and dreams restored is the greatest joy of my life!

I want you to experience the joy I have had from mentoring...it's amazing how good it feels to help people 'get unstuck' from areas I used to be stuck in. It makes me so thankful for the hard times, because God has used them all to help others. Don't let your pain and healing go to waste... 'take someone with you' on this journey.

MICHELLE E. CASWELL   PURELY HIS, INC.

Let's Talk About It

1. Where could you begin volunteering in Purely His, your church or another ministry that has a heart for the same type of people you do?

_____

_____

_____

_____

_____

2. Are you feeling more equipped to serve and mentor others?

_____

_____

_____

_____

3. Do you feel hesitant or excited to mentor? Why?

_____

_____

_____

_____

Let's Take Action

Homework

- Write out your testimony within two pages. You could likely write a book about your life, but for now, stay with the short version. This is just a rough draft so don't stress over it. It's important to get good at knowing 'your story' and telling it. It's a very effective tool for mentoring. The Bible says "be quick to give a response when someone asks why you have hope" (1Peter 3:15).

- Contact a person from your group and tell them one way that you have seen them grow in the past several months.

MICHELLE E. CASWELL   PURELY HIS, INC.

Let's Reflect

Tell Your Story in 2 pages or less.

To be continued. The best is yet to come...

Week 21 – Part of Something Bigger

"Go into ALL the world and make disciples of ALL men"
Matthew 28:19

Purely His is going to be a world-wide ministry because we are taking the Great Commission serious-ly and we would love for you to join us in that effort. This group is designed to make disciples that make disciples, that make disciples…and there are many ways to do that. For those that do decide to join us by leading a group, further training is available to equip you. I would love for you to lead a group for Purely His at least one time to solidify what you have learned but also pass along all you have learned.

But one thing is for sure, the friendships you have developed in this group will last forever. You can't go through this deep healing with each other and not stay connected. However, it takes ef-fort to maintain relationships, so make sure you make the effort. It's worth it.

Take your rightful place in the kingdom by sharing all the Lord has done in your life. You have survived and now you are ready to thrive.

This is the last time your group will be meeting once a week. Make a time once a month that you can all get together for a while or at least four times a year. Make sure to keep in touch with each other because having accountability and support is so important to 'get unstuck" and stay unstuck.

Think about the times you've said or thought *"If I had known then what I know now, I would have made a different decision."* GO! Share this with someone; so that you can save them a lot of time and heartache. Take what you've been learning and GO make a difference in this world. Go love God and people by making disciples!

Let's Talk About It

1. Keeping in mind the spiritual gifts you have and the desires in your heart, how would you like to be a part of the bigger picture of Purely His?

   _____

   _____

   _____

   _____

   _____

2. What have you learned that you will be taking with you?

   _____

   _____

   _____

   _____

3. What are your famous last words to us?

   _____

   _____

   _____

   _____

MICHELLE E. CASWELL   PURELY HIS, INC.

Let's Take Action

Homework

- Read through this workbook or the journal you used during the group and see how much you've grown and then write an entry about your growth.

- Contact someone this week and tell them what area of their life you have seen them grow the most.

Let's Reflect

What are you feeling or experiencing as your five months has come to an end?
Did you grow in the Lord...did you heal...are you more free now?

_____

_____

_____

_____

_____

_____

_____

_____

_____

_____

_____

_____

_____

_____

_____

Your Story doesn't end here...this is just the beginning.....

MICHELLE E. CASWELL   PURELY HIS, INC.

Notes

_____

_____

_____

_____

_____

_____

_____

_____

_____

_____

_____

_____

_____

_____

_____

_____

_____

Your Story doesn't end here…this is just the beginning…..

Notes

Your Story doesn't end here...this is just the beginning.....

MICHELLE E. CASWELL   PURELY HIS, INC.

Notes

_____

_____

_____

_____

_____

_____

_____

_____

_____

_____

_____

_____

_____

_____

_____

_____

Your Story doesn't end here...this is just the beginning.....

Notes

_____

_____

_____

_____

_____

_____

_____

_____

_____

_____

_____

_____

_____

_____

_____

_____

_____

_____

Your Story doesn't end here...this is just the beginning.....

MICHELLE E. CASWELL   PURELY HIS, INC.

Author Michelle E. Caswell is the wife of Matt, mom of Stefan and Jordan and two step daughters, Kirsten and Kaeleigh and the grandmother to Hunter. She is the author of "Calling All Workers" and the founder and president of Purely His, Inc. She spent the first thirty years of her life living for herself and all the world had to offer, but she now lives her life 'sold out' to Jesus and is determined to finish strong in Him. She has been forgiven of a sixteen year sex addiction, drug addiction and alcoholism, two divorces, two abortions, neglecting her kids, lying, stealing and the list goes on. BUT God chose to forgive her, set her free and now uses her story mightily to help people learn how to go all in with Jesus and get unstuck from anything in the way of that.